T0132034

PIP'S

MEMOIRS and MANOEUVRES

PAUL GABRIEL

© 2021 Paul Gabriel. All rights reserved.

No part of this book may be reproduced, stored in a retrieval system, or transmitted by any means without the written permission of the author.

AuthorHouse™ UK
1663 Liberty Drive
Bloomington, IN 47403 USA
www.authorhouse.co.uk
UK TFN: 0800 0148641 (Toll Free inside the UK)
UK Local: 02036 956322 (+44 20 3695 6322 from outside the UK)

Because of the dynamic nature of the Internet, any web addresses or links contained in this book may have changed since publication and may no longer be valid. The views expressed in this work are solely those of the author and do not necessarily reflect the views of the publisher, and the publisher hereby disclaims any responsibility for them.

Any people depicted in stock imagery provided by Getty Images are models, and such images are being used for illustrative purposes only.
Certain stock imagery © Getty Images.

This book is printed on acid-free paper.

ISBN: 978-1-6655-8515-6 (sc)
ISBN: 978-1-6655-8516-3 (e)

Print information available on the last page.

Published by AuthorHouse 01/28/2021

authorHOUSE®

A blue MGB soft-top rattled to rest just in front of a low-level stone wall. The driver adjusted his peak cap and got out, making his way to the front door of the corner section of a U-shaped property called Angel Court. He rang the bell and waited. As the door opened, faces lit up with smiles all round.

'Hi! How are you, Aunt?' said the driver. 'Long time, no see!'

'Yes, Robert, my dear. It has been a while. But anyway, we are all fine. Come on in and have a cup of tea!'

'Oh! Well, good timing then!' Robert laughed and crossed the threshold, making his way into the sitting room just behind a narrow hallway. 'I was just on my way back to London and hoped you might be in.'

'It's lovely to see you. Have a seat.'

Robert settled into one of two armchairs and placed his arms on the armrests. 'So, anyway, I was just wondering if Pip would like to come back to London with me and stay for a while.'

'Just a mo while I call him. He's upstairs.'

I'd overheard the conversation and came downstairs. 'Hi, Robert. What brings you to our neck of the woods? Have you come to take me away?'

'Just thought you'd like some time in London—maybe find a job, enjoy a bit of London life!'

'That sounds like fun. Yes, please,' I said.

A cup of tea and a chat later, I packed a case, and we set off. About an hour later, we hit the London traffic. We eventually arrived at Regents Park, where Robert parked the car. We then had a short walk to Ridinghouse Street where the flat was.

'Blimey,' I said, 'enough stairs! I suppose you have the top flat?'

'Quite right, sprout. Onward and upward.'

We finally reached the front door and entered. Almost immediately in front was the entrance to a very small kitchen, which boasted a tabletop that folded down on top of the bath. This was a useful area on which many fine cakes were made and some of the finest raw eggs whisked up in glasses of milk, making breakfast very quick! Any further culinary expertise in the cooking line was performed on the gas cooker opposite the bath. Here a good old-fashioned fry-up or lamb chops might be the order of the day.

Beyond the kitchen was a doorway that led to an old-fashioned loo with a chain pull. A small window at high level let the nasty whiffs outside, while all manner of insects invaded the inside. Out of the kitchen, an immediate turn left led into the bedroom, with just enough room for a double bed and a wardrobe. Turn left out of the bedroom, and the sitting room welcomed you to a comfy sofa, a TV, and a rug on the fitted carpet. In one corner, extending the length of one side was a large window seat, which would be my bed. It was a long drop to the street below. I shuddered!

I spent a few days visiting likely places of work—*Daily Mail*; Felden Advertising; in fact, any newspaper and any advertising agency.

After several days of, 'Sorry, we don't have any positions free at present,' I decided to send a letter to Arthur Sanderson & Sons in Berners Street. My sister had worked there six years ago, and this helped me get an interview, which went very well. In fact, a phone call later, I had a job! Money wasn't great, but commission and overtime would bump up the pay packet.

It was only a ten-minute walk to Sanderson & Sons, so I didn't have to get up that early. My first day at the showroom, I was shown round with an Australian girl, also just starting. This girl was particularly funny, with her broad accent and 'outback' stories, which were told on Friday nights in the local pub.

The showroom floor was quite long. Banks of screens showed all the different wallpapers, producing a *clatter, clatter* sound as they were flicked through by the customers. Sometimes the noise was deafening.

❦

Sue McCulloch joined the sales team a few months after me. She was from South Africa, and we became 'just good friends'. She had a great sense of humour and an infectious laugh. One day I asked her if she would like a trip to Paris with me with a view to having lunch at the top of the Eiffel Tower. She looked at me warily, thinking I was having her on. And when she discovered I wasn't, she laughed and said yes!

I picked her up the following Saturday, and we flew to Orly Airport. We were at the top of the Eiffel Tower by 1.30 p.m.—in time for lunch and a chance to take in magnificent views all round. We visited Notre Dame and took a couple of trips on the metro, just to compare with the London Underground. We got lost briefly but found our way back eventually.

The evening's entertainment was a restaurant local to the hotel, where I excelled in choosing from the French menu—*sole meunière* for Sue and *steak tartare* for me. Trouble was, I had no idea that my meal was minced cold beef! Another glass of wine helped to ease my embarrassment. We both laughed!

We clung to each other as we walked back to our hotel and took the lift up to our room. Soon we were there. And if you're wondering if we did it, the answer is no—I fell asleep almost immediately!

After breakfast the next morning, we paid the bill and left our luggage with reception while we took a final stroll before catching the bus to the airport. We both had good fun!

❦

I was at Sanderson & Sons for three years and learnt a good deal about wallpapers, paints, and general interior design. I taught myself how to paper and the right way to paint. All this would stand me in good stead.

I was lucky enough to meet several celebrities, some of whom required my help in choosing the right wallpapers. Jackie Pallo, the wrestler known as Mr TV, and his wife, Trixie, made my job easy—they just wanted everything purple! Even easier was Jimmy Tarbuck, who wanted a roll of cork paper. And would I drop it round to his Regent Street office? Judi Dench and Ian Hendry were just browsing. Danny La Rue wanted wallpaper for his recent acquisition—the Swan Hotel in Goring. The Duke of St Albans didn't think he should put his address on the back of his cheque but did anyway.

Sheila Steafel, formerly married to Harry H. Corbett, came to the showroom to choose papers and paints for her home, which was being featured in a glossy magazine. I was picked as 'delivery boy', since I lived just round the corner in the bigger flat that Robert and I had moved to. The more I went to see Sheila, the more the friendship blossomed, and she asked me to do some woodwork in her downstairs loo, which worked out well. She gave me a free ticket to one of her recorded TV shows. After that, the phone stopped ringing—she was busy, and I had found someone else.

Jim Chapman was the floor manager and limped around the showroom with a stick. He enjoyed a good joke and was well liked by everyone. I remember a couple of occasions when he passed me on the showroom floor, muttering 'You randy old stoat!'

It was all good-natured, but I asked him where he got his facts from. We laughed!

By now, I was beginning to feel I could do quite well as a self-employed decorator, as I had learnt so much. In fact, a good customer of mine rang me up to suggest leaving Sanderson and doing just that! So I handed in my notice and ordered some flashy black cards with gold printing on. 'The randy old stoat' was moving on!

I rang a friend of mine named Mike to tell him I was now self-employed, and within a week, he phoned me to say that a couple of his friends were moving into a flat in his block. They needed a decorator. I was duly summoned and was asked to paint the whole flat and to remove the fire surround and block up the hole. We sorted out finances, and I told them I could start straightaway.

I soon pulled the fire surround away from the wall and made good—after a ton of bricks and soot had descended! I bagged it all up and took it downstairs to the concierge's flat, whereupon he told me not to leave the bag outside his flat.

'You need a skip, mate—you can't leave it here!

'But Mike told me you would dispose of it. What if I slipped you a tenner?'

'Oh! Go on then. Leave it to muggins.'

So with all the rubbish taken care of, I got on with decorating the rooms, fitting a new kitchen, and tiling the bathroom. The Lovell-Smiths liked what I had done and said they would recommend me.

During my first assignment, I had been driving an olive-green Triumph Vitesse. This was not a good thing, as it was totally impractical for carting tools and equipment. So I phoned a friend at Sanderson, and he offered me £250 for it, which I accepted. Now I was in a position to buy a white minivan from Holbein Motors. This was a cool move, as well as sensible.

I put some black tumble-twist rugs in the back to soften the hollowness of the space. One or two friends passed slightly ambiguous comments. But then, what are friends for?

The new flat in West Hampstead was a dream come true! There were four bedrooms, a kitchen, a bathroom, a large sitting room, and a spacious entrance hall.

My cousin worked in the theatre as stage manager and quite often was away on tour. So looking after the flat was left to me. Tim Curry, an aspiring actor, occupied one of the rooms and seemed to be permanently cold—which often resulted in him running a hot bath and sitting in it!!

Joan Armatrading had just left the musical *Hair* and was busy writing songs that would make her a star. She amused me by quite often using the words 'get off', which you might think meant literally 'get off me' but actually meant 'rubbish'.

Adrian Digtham was a bit of a theatre technician. He filled the only vacant room and arrived at the flat with quad speakers capable of waking the dead as well as taking up all the floor space!

❦

My next challenge was a delicatessen at the top of Beauchamp Place in Knightsbridge. This was quite a prestigious job to have, bearing in mind the location. The boss there was Didier Milinaire, who is related to the Duchess of Bedford. He was great fun to work for, and I managed to weave my way round the customers with not too many paint spots!

He then asked me to decorate the outside washroom with some imitation tiles on hardboard backing. I managed to bang a nail into a cold water pipe, which was not a good move—especially since I couldn't move, as my finger was pressed onto the hole. I could only shout for help! Luckily Didier heard me and switched the water off until a plumber had been summoned. What a relief!

Lynn, a friend of mine (who insisted on calling me sugar plum) got me my next job building cupboards and decorating for a 'jingles' company in Piccadilly. The music that surrounded me while I was working spurred me on to give songwriting a shot in the evenings. I was proficient in playing guitar but only knew four chords!

Lynn got in touch again to say she was moving out of her flat in Battersea and I should go down there to meet the new girl who was moving in. So I did. One evening I went down and met them all playing a game called Sorry. Then all the lights went out, and confusion reigned for a few moments. I was able to talk with Rosemary, the incoming flatmate and decided fairly quickly she was the one!

I was not feeling very confident, so I asked several of the girls to meet me at a local pub. This way it wouldn't seem like I was rushing. But only Rosemary came, so c'est la vie. She liked me too, even though I was rather conceited! She went off skiing with her family for a fortnight, and we both felt the same when she returned. Love had truly struck!

Then came the big party at Prince of Wales mansions thrown by all the girls in the flat! Unfortunately I was very late because I had fallen asleep. Never has anyone driven so quickly from West Hampstead to Battersea! I was forgiven!

I started moving around the room meeting new people, including Bill Martin, the songwriter, responsible for writing 'Puppet on a String', 'Congratulations', and many more. Jan was his lady-love, and they were about to get married. And with that in mind, they asked me to decorate a house they had bought in Fulham. This was a great follow-up to my previous jobs and I managed to get a lot of the work done while they were on honeymoon. The remainder of the work was completed about three weeks later.

No sooner had I finished this house than Bill asked me to decorate another house in Weybridge. This was a beautiful place, with pretty gardens and room for a swimming pool! I decorated all the rooms and, pretty soon, was able to steer my stepladders in a different direction.

I got a call from my brother-in-law, Richard, telling me he and his co-directors, BFMOS for short, were moving to a first-floor office in one of the old buildings in Great Peter Street. They wanted a false ceiling down the passageway and three rooms decorated. Some wallpaper was required for the reception desk area. This area was controlled by a lovely lady called Zoë, who hid behind a haze of cigarette smoke. (A nickname, 'Fagash', seemed appropriate!)

The job went well, and Zoë was going to prove very useful in passing work my way. In fact, she rang me soon after I finished my work at the offices of BFMOS. She and Reg had bought a house in Clapham, and she wanted me to decorate throughout and reshuffle the kitchen. The next five weeks were busy, but job done.

※

I married Rosemary on 15 June 1974 on a gloriously sunny day. The church was next door to the Penrose house and gardens, so the setting was perfect. About a hundred guests made the whole event a lot of fun. Even the vicar smiled!

Our first home was a furnished flat in Marloes Road, London. And that's where we were heading after Rosemary's mother tapped her watch and said, 'Now come along, you two. It's time to go!' Bossy boots!

With our little mini in shiny damask red, tinted windows, and a loo roll hanging on the exhaust pipe, we were finally off amid good wishes and clapping. What a day!

Home 1

We arrived back in London and parked just outside our flat. No one knew we were there except Rosemary's cousin, who lived in the flat above. We had cancelled our honeymoon in Sark, as it was going to take too many stopovers to get there. The dame would have to wait a bit longer for our custom.

A week's honeymoon, and it was back to work for Rosemary but not for me, as I had no immediate work on hand. This changed after I did a small job down in Liphook, Surrey. The phone started to ring again, and I was back in business!

Home 2

The following year, we decided to look for our first house and drove off to Hampton Hill. We found a semi-detached 1930s style house that required complete decoration and fitted cupboards, as well as knocking two rooms into one. With all that in mind, we offered £12,000, and our offer was accepted.

Bushey Park was just across the road from our house, so we walked there with our Jack Russell, Fidget, as often as we could.

At a party in Fulham, we met up with Tim and Jo Webster, who indirectly knew Rosemary's family, the Penroses. Tim was about to leave the Duke of Edinburgh Award scheme in favour of becoming self-employed as a carpenter/joiner. At the outset, we really hit it off, and so did Rosemary with Jo. Rosemary was about to become self-employed as a cordon bleu cook, as she had been awarded a certificate from her cooking school. Jo was keen to help with dinner parties and weddings, with me as chief butler and bottle washer! What a great team!

Tim and I joined forces on various jobs, the first of which was fairly local to me in Sunbury. We were asked to build some small offices within a large office and then carry out the decorations. It all worked out very well. And Peter Knight, the designer, was very pleased with the outcome.

❧

My brother-in-law was in touch again. This time, he was asking me to have a go at producing a thirty-second commercial advertising Swan and Edgar in Piccadilly. Wow! That's amazing—yes, please!

I met up with Richard at Emison, an offshoot from EMI. And there I was shown the recording studios and met up with guitarist Bill Aitken and Paul Deeley, chief engineer and a nice bloke!

We came up with the required jingle, but Gary Osborne came up with a better one! Never mind. Stick around and wait for the next one.

Actually that was not too far ahead. A chap called. Stevie Meryke asked for some identity music for Penine Radio. I was successful this time, and an advance cheque for £100 really made me feel a sense of achievement.

❧

Tim and I returned to working together—this time at Jacksons of Piccadilly! This was a prestigious job and financially rewarding. When all was finished, Tim and Jo were going on holiday, and so were we.

Rosemary was going up to Scotland with a friend to cook for a shooting party, and I was going to Cornwall to join my sister and family. Tim lent me his gold-coloured VW, which had quite a throaty roar but was very comfortable.

I reached St Merryn in Cornwall just in the nick of time. I had an awful stomach ache. Just by chance, there was an outside washroom, and the family were out! Say no more.

Home 3

On return from holiday, Rosemary and I discussed selling our house and looking for a Victorian semi-detached home in Teddington. We put our house on the market and almost immediately had an offer of £19,000, which was great! We managed to find a Victorian semi in Teddington, which was on the market for £19,000 also. We offered the asking price, and that was accepted. Things were suddenly moving quickly. We asked our solicitor to deal with the conveyancing on both houses at the same time, and that worked well.

Rosemary's parents came down with horsebox and trailer and helped us move, which was very helpful and, obviously, saved us a lot of money.

The first major thing to organise was the rewiring. John Penrose, Rosemary's dad, came down to do it for us—so generous and kind. While he was with us, he told me that the boss of the Brewers Guild in London was wanting fresh decorations for his offices. So I made an appointment to meet Harrington and to see what needed to be done. Everything was straightforward and subject to me showing Harrington something I had done. The job was mine!

Tim and I had worked together again on a firm of solicitors' offices, so this was the obvious place to show off. I phoned Harrington, and we met there.

The meeting was successful. 'Start as soon as you can,' he said as we parted, smiling.

I did quite a bit of decorating in the evenings when I got back from London but soon discovered that a break now and then is important. This is where gin and tonic came my way fairly often when the going got tough! The job at the Brewers Guild soon ended with thanks all round and a thought that I might have a few days to myself!

The phone rang, and it was Zoë saying they had bought another house. Would I like to decorate it for them? I went to have a look and gave them a price and a starting date.

In the meantime, I decided we should knock down the chimney breast in our dining room, which was fine, but then we should do the same in the bedroom. It was now time to call on a bricky friend called Bill, who used to be a prize fighter or similar, and he showed me how to strut the brickwork in the roof so the struts would bear the weight. Then we could knock the bricks out in the bedroom. It's easy when you know how.

We put in for planning permission to build a single-storey extension to the kitchen, which was approved the second time around. While we waited for builders to be available, I made a start on Zoë's house and decorated from top to bottom. And I heard from Zoë that her friends Linda and Godfrey Morrow wanted their house done just like Zoë's. It took a while to finish Zoë's house, but when it was finished it really looked good!

No builders yet, so I made a start on Linda and Godfrey's house. About halfway through, I was knocked over by a motorbike, a Kawasaki 1000, ridden by Gary Musto. I woke up in hospital with two policemen peering down on me. I was unable to help, so they left. I was in hospital for five days before they let me go home.

Linda was now chasing me to finish her job, so I employed two decorator friends of mine, George and Steve, to help knock the job on the head, as it were. Soon I was back home, and builders were about to start. A deposit of £500 was needed to get the job underway, but although footings were being dug, and equipment was on site, it was difficult to pin our builder down. We discovered he had a penchant for betting shops. We had one or two upsets, but when the extension was finished, it looked great!

I made my first kitchen for our extension and then laid Amtico tiles for the first time. And before you could say no, we were ready for Peter, our friendly milkman who was going to lay our dark brown carpets.

What joy when all was done!

Once again, we decided to put our house on the market. But this time, we advertised it in our local paper for £50,000. The fifth couple to come round offered to pay the asking price. Fantastic!

Home 4

My brother rang to congratulate us and to advise us to buy the freehold in a block of flats in Hindhead, Surrey. After a bit of thought, we agreed. Once again, our solicitor did two conveyancings at the same time!

Zoë rang again to say she and Reg had bought another house in Clapham. This time, I suggested she ask Rosemary's brother, Nutty Nick, to do the honours. I would be around, though, if needed.

Well, it wasn't long before I was needed. I met up with everyone in Clapham and immediately saw the problem with the wallpaper design. Cherries do not grow upwards. Nutty Nick maintained that they do, so we all laughed—except Nick, who threw in the towel and walked off the job. I took over to finish the job off properly. Problem solved.

Home 5

We moved ourselves and all our possessions down to the flat in Hindhead. It was a spacious place with plenty of room for everything. All we had to do was build cupboards and decorate everywhere! We even knocked a hole through the sitting room wall to the sun lounge, which gave us an extra bedroom and sitting room. We had a dispute with the builder, who maintained no RSJ was necessary. We said it was. He still persevered with his invoice, and in the end, our solicitors told us to pay it. Like good little children we obeyed!

Another builder came and put the job right. Once again, we put our home on the market and managed to get an acceptable offer. We then found an idyllic cottage on Kingsley Common near Alton, Hampshire. Our offer on that was accepted. And pretty soon, we were ensconced in our new home. There was a fair amount of work to do—new staircase, new front and rear doors and frames, and complete decorations

When it was finished we had achieved complete cosiness! It is known as the Manse. We spent a lot of time investigating the Common, which was on our doorstep. It was heavily used by the MOD for training purposes. Where have I heard that before?

Home 6

On one of our walks, we discovered an old colonial-style bungalow in among tall grasses and shielded by several trees. *What a fabulous place*, we thought and talked about it non-stop on our way back to our cottage. 'I wonder who owns it?' I questioned.

We discovered it was Nora Richardson. She lived in London and came to stay at weekends with her husband, who, sadly, had recently died. She had just put the bungalow on the market, with planning permission for a new dwelling. She told us she would love to sell to us and not a local builder. So we arranged to meet her there to look around. We loved what we saw and could see a new house might be better on a different part of the garden. Anyway, for now we said we would like to buy it. She agreed to let us have a mortgage but might need to ask for it back sooner rather than later.

Our cottage went on the market. Fairly quickly, we had an acceptable offer, which meant, once again, we could instruct our solicitor to deal with two conveyances.

About the time of moving to the Manse, we had been giving the desire for children some thought—as well as practise! Various tests had shown we probably would not have children in the normal way. So IVF was recommended but failed at the first, second, and third fence. We decided to go for adoption, and we were in touch with social services before we left the Manse. We passed all the necessary questions connected with adoption, and we agreed to be back in touch as soon as we had moved.

After we had been in the bungalow for a couple of weeks, we arranged for one of the members of social services to come out and look at our surroundings. We explained we would be building a new house but elsewhere in the garden, not on the same site. As far as the social services need know, the bungalow would be quite adequate to bring up children. When the new home was ready, everything would fall into place. I think social services could tell we were quite serious about everything. It was just a matter of when.

We met up with an architect called Mike, who came up with some pretty impressive drawings, which we agreed to and left it to him to organise the footings and a pipe run to a septic tank. Mike told us he had had three quotes for digging the footings, and the best was for £10,000, so we said go ahead. Paul Old, the builder, started the job fairly quickly, and three weeks later, the job was done.

I plumbed in a loo in the bungalow. And just before the builder was ready to leave, I asked him to connect up my waste from the loo to the septic tank, leaving us a blanking plate when it came to moving into the new house. Job done.

Social services came out to us again to see progress, if any! They were pleasantly surprised to see the outline of the new house and to see the organisation of the bungalow. I did say to them it would be best to finish the new house before we did anything family-wise. In their eyes, of course, that could be a long time. And also, if a child came up for adoption, you couldn't expect the procedure to wait while bricks were being laid!

The days rolled by, with Rosemary making cakes and jams to sell locally and to anyone who called from the village. I was asked to renovate a bathroom in Oakhanger for a lovely family called Kilner, who kindly passed my name onto several other people. They often bought cakes from Rosemary, so it was a great way to make friends.

It was time for the next phase of our house—the oversite. Truckloads of ready-mixed concrete arrived and got laid, as it were. Soon the area of our new house was awash with concrete—massive!

We had a call from social services to say that a family of three had come into care, and they thought that we would be ideal parents. We went to meet them and were shown into a room where we sat at the back so we could observe from a distance. The two girls came in chattering away and looking rather stressed, which was only to be expected, since their young mother had just died, aged twenty-three. We fell in love with them almost immediately and agreed to look after them and Daniel, who was only seven months old and still with his foster mother.

We had several picnics in the garden of our bungalow over a period of two months and then set a date when we would take Daniel for a couple of weeks on his own before the girls came. I do not remember how we felt when the children came to us—probably in a state of shock! Just like that we were a family of five! Various young members of the village came to help Rosemary so I could get back to work.

I met up with a beautiful lady called Gaye who wanted masses of decorating done in her house. And Freddie, her husband, wanted masses done in his offices in Weybridge. I was with them both for the next three months, which meant we could do more to help the construction of our new house. Magic!

So with all this work on my plate, I could employ Trevor and Stuart Coles to build up the walls to wall plate level and to fit the glulam beams, which were specially ordered from Sweden. These had to be hoisted into place by a crane and really made the house look enormous! The Coles brothers' work was now finished, and we made inroads into a larger mortgage to get the roof tiled, which we were able to do.

I was lucky enough to pick up two new kitchens in the village. I was then in a position to order all our windows and doors. Now it was all coming together!

One gloriously sunny morning, the children woke us up early. As was customary, much laughter came from their room, usually meaning they had thrown something somewhere or had made some funny noises. Anyway, before we let them into our room, Rosemary quite calmly announced she was pregnant! This came as quite a shock, as well as fantastic news. So I could father children after all. Well, celebrations all round! Rosemary's mother phoned to ask me what I had been doing. And I replied that, if she didn't know by now, I wasn't the one who should tell her!

The next few months were very busy. We had organised Daisy and Vicki to go to playgroup most mornings, which left Daniel in his playpen and then a walk across the common. Rosemary was in her element. Our lives were changing! The roof of the house was now being tiled, and the windows and doors were also being fitted. All we needed was the glass to make us weather tight. And this was completed after the windows were fitted.

We were fairly slow in making progress with the other tradespeople. We had rendering, plastering, plumbing and electrics, and carpentry. The most important manoeuvre was the rendering. With this done, the outside of the house would be finished. The plasterers then finished inside the house, which meant screeding the floors, as well as plastering the partition walls upstairs. What a difference it was making.

The electrician had laid all his cables and had decided where to position his fuse box. The plumber came along and laid all his pipework, with a view to connecting all the sanitary ware when tiling and decorating was finished. I had ordered a preformed staircase to suit our opening, and a local carpenter came to fit it.

I was quite keen to move into the new house before our baby was born, so I did quite a lot of evening work on the bedrooms getting them ready for decorating. Rupert, my nephew, was primed to come in and do a spell of painting to make our target more attainable. Once the painting was complete, the electrician came in to second fix switches and socket plates. And the plumber started connecting up all the sanitary ware. Now we were motoring, or cooking on gas—whichever you prefer!

It was possible now to move in in the knowledge that there were still a lot of things to do. But I was thinking about Rosemary and the baby. We did move in. Of course, Rosemary's mother was coming to stay. And funny to look back on it now, but when she arrived, Rosemary yelled, 'We need to go!'

Action stations, and off we went in the van to the military hospital at Aldershot. Rosemary was rushed in to the delivery room, and almost immediately, Georgie was born. How brilliant was that! I was asked to cut the umbilical cord. Then I went to the waiting room, where a sergeant told me to move my van quickly, or it would be removed and blown up!

Rosemary's mother was an absolute brick and stayed for a few days until we said we were ready to cope. She then left us to it! The girls were settled in their playgroup, Daniel was now walking and happy to play in his pen for some of the time, and Georgina cried a bit and slept a bit. Our black Labrador was just happy to be lying down wherever he chose to be. This was our new routine. This was our biggest manoeuvre of all!

I was asked to renovate a kitchen in the village, and this led to a very happy relationship between us and the Rentons. They let us use their pool whenever it was fine—so generous.

I then had a run of three kitchens to make—one in Farnham, one in Rowledge, and one make-and-deliver, only to a London address. All this work meant we could pay back our loan from Mrs Richardson, which made me feel better.

We managed to get a bit of landscape garden done. So in a few months, the children had somewhere to run about in safety.

Otherwise, life continued to be busy—getting to know the children and to love them, watching them with their friends, coping with schooling, and listening to them whine at us when we said no. Georgina, occasionally, would fly off the handle and say to whoever was annoying her, 'Stink bomb willy face, pah.' I believe it was mostly aimed at Daniel!

We fought the council over the bungalow and won the right to keep it.

What was not quite such good news was we still couldn't make enough money to stay in our new house, and we couldn't find a buyer. However, some friends of ours from the neighbouring common asked us if we would care to swap, which we agreed to very quickly. What was really good about the manoeuvre was we really liked their house. There was plenty of room for all of us and a lovely garden. Also, there was a useful workshop at the bottom of the garden. So we were manoeuvring again!

The cottage we live in now.

Modern House in Kingstone after Little Headlands Farm

Little Headlands Farm after we sold our Barn conversion

Flatts Farm

Swallow Barn before conversion

The School House

Manse Cottage- 1st house on Kingsley Common- Moved here when we sold our flat

Bungalows on Kingsley

Footings for new house in Kingsley Common

Next Stage after footings

3rd stage

4th stage

Job done

Chimney Breast Removed

House in Teddington

Victorian Semi Detached in Teddington. Our Second Home.

Home 8

I do have to mention the fire. I came back from work and spotted a thin spiral of smoke coming from Rosemary's car. I rushed in to tell her, but she didn't think it was that serious. Five minutes later, and it was serious!

I called the fire brigade, who arrived within minutes and didn't take long to soak our car and our drive. Then the police arrived and asked if we had any enemies. Enemies—I ask you! Anyway the loss adjuster came and agreed it was a write-off and took pictures and made notes.

We were then sent a cheque, which enabled us to buy a Volvo.

I needed to put electricity down in the workshop and called out a couple of electricians. This was not without its drama. One of the electricians drilled unto the mains cable, causing his hair to stand on end, a large shrivelled-up drill bit hanging from his drill. So we were without electricity until a linesman could come out and renew the cable. Once this was done, we could get back to normal. What a relief!

Now the workshop was fully operational I could carry on making an old pine kitchen for some friends of ours. He ran his own business called Designs Direct, so he had produced some really useful plans for me to follow. When completed, it all looked smashing!

Next job was quite a manoeuvre in itself. I was asked to make ten lots of the same furniture—bedside table and drawer, wardrobe, and desk. All were to be delivered and fitted in a student block of flats. No one spoke any English, so I talked to myself.

The children were progressing well at school and showing varying interests. Daniel was learning the piano and, at the age of four, played Joseph in his playgroup play. With so many house moves under our belts, we were running out of money. We talked about moving again just to clear our debts. This time, we thought about shifting up to the Midlands. It would probably be cheaper there. Workwise I wasn't too sure how easy that might be. Only one way to find out! We decided to give it a go.

We put our house on the market and sold well. Question now was where to go until we found something up in the Midlands. Wendy Renton came to our rescue and let us stay in her mother's house, which was being sold. We moved lock, stock, and tennis rackets and then started to make plans about the Midlands.

Rosemary and Daniel went up to Burton upon Trent to look for a house and found one fairly quickly called the School House, near Sudbury. Rosemary told me it was next to the railway line but thought we could handle that. She had put in an offer, so I thought I'd better go and look. She came back, and I went up the following day.

Home 9

The rooms in the School House were spacious, especially upstairs. So I could see how to turn the biggest room into two rooms, which would mean the children would all have their own room. Downstairs there was a large dining room, sitting room, and kitchen with a downstairs loo and washbasin. Yes, it would be fine for all of us. So I drove back to the family with thumbs up, and we chased our solicitor to complete the conveyancing!

While we waited for completion, we organised Rosemary's mother to house the family while I knocked the house into shape. Paul Russell came up and stayed in the house while he replumbed the whole place, including heating. Derek came and rewired the property, so floorboards were up everywhere. It was chaos but short-lived.

I was upstairs building a partition in the biggest room, turning it into two rooms. At the end of three weeks, we had new functioning bathroom and kitchen, new heating, and new electrics. I managed to do the decorating and suggested to the family that we should move in. So we did!

We needed to sort out schooling for the family, which was a good reason for coming up to the Midlands. Boarding school would be best if we could get some help in the form of a bursary for each. Abbots Bromley invited us for tea, so Rosemary, myself, Daisy, and Vicki settled into the headmaster's sitting room and enjoyed tea. Daisy and Vicki fought over the biscuit tin, so I thought that was the end of that.

However, a letter from the headmaster said, 'We will try and educate your daughter.' So Vicki was fixed up.

Now to find a school for Daisy. We went to Abbotsholme and felt that this would suit her very well. Outside activities were ideal for her.

Daniel and Georgina went to Richard Wakefield School in Tutbury as day pupils.

I started to use the workshop in the estate office, and with some of our furniture now back at our house, I could set up some display kitchens. My suppliers of kitchen doors sent me a letter telling me they were discontinuing a range of old pine doors. Was I interested? Yes, I was. I offered £1,100 for the whole lot—about three hundred items. Over a period of fifteen months, I made and sold fifteen kitchens using all the old pine doors. It was a profitable time for me, and I certainly needed it.

A girl called Annie came to my workshop and told me she lived in Edinburgh and was visiting her mum in Littleover just round the corner from me. She wanted me to make an old pine kitchen for her using a floor plan and photographs—which encouraged me to say yes! Once terms had been agreed, I made a start. It took about two weeks to make, and then I was ready to manoeuvre. I stayed in a bed and breakfast round the corner from Annie, and when it was all completed, they took me out to dinner! It had all gone so well!

Once I was back home, I persevered with setting up more displays, which continued to sell well, enabling me to finish our home. We decided to put up a conservatory, which completed the outside look of the place.

It wasn't long before we decided we needed more space outside, so we put the house on the market. We found a farm just outside Uttoxeter called Flatts farm. We went to take a look, and it was amazing! How much? How *much*!

I needed to juggle figures, and we hadn't actually sold our present home. But when we did, I put in an offer for the farm, and it was accepted. Fantastic! I organised a non-status mortgage, and we were on manoeuvres again. This was going to be as big a project as our house that we'd built in Kingsley.

Home 10

We put in new windows and rewired the place. And apart from decorating everywhere that was all we did! Outside, there were four stables and two open barns, which I used for my kitchen displays.

The children all wanted to ride ponies. So we borrowed four ponies from different quarters. Daniel didn't last long, as he didn't want to muck out or clean tack. Daisy dropped out because boyfriends were more exciting. Georgie gave up. And Vicki kept going but not with us. She left home to live with her boyfriend and continued riding there.

It occurred to me that all the outbuildings would make a lovely home for someone. And so I applied for planning permission once we had some plans drawn up. We were successful.

We decided to do the conversion ourselves, and so we employed Mike Hudson, our builder from School House days, and he stripped the roof and re-felted, and battered before replacing the tiles. Then he concreted the floors to a mirror finish, so we wouldn't have to screed on top. He finished by repointing all the brickwork. All the windows were made and fitted. Inside, all the walls were dry lined and then plastered. The whole place was plumbed, and new electrics connected up. I put in a new hand-painted kitchen.

Home 11

When all this was done, we decided we would move in to it and sell the farmhouse. So we sold the farmhouse to a speculator who had sold his mobile phone business. But he in turn didn't stay long and sold to another mobile phone millionaire. Rosemary didn't want to stay in our barn conversion. So we sent a letter to the brother of the new owner of the farm, asking him if he would like to buy ours. He did, and we had no agents' fees. So we had done rather well!

HOME 12

ventually, we found another farm for sale in Withington, which was ideal for us. We put up a large workshop in the field next to the house and replaced all the windows. I put in an old pine kitchen, and we invested in a second-hand AGA. Our next-door neighbour, who was a builder, connected us to the main drainage system, and Mike Hudson renovated a dilapidated shed so Georgina could have a dance studio.

Our family was now all leaving school and wanting jobs. Alton Towers employed them all from time to time, until two of the family decided to go to Australia and New Zealand.

We had the most amazing party to celebrate my sixtieth birthday and brought in a traditional Jazz band, plus eighty guests and a big pan of stew!

I had a shock letter from the bank asking me to repay a large sum of money I had borrowed and to refrain from using my account except for urgent every day things.

We were on manoeuvres once again. We never seemed able to spend more than three years in any one place.

Home 13

We sold the farm well and paid the bank what we owed. We were then able to buy a modern house in Kingstone for cash. We then took some equity from the house so we could get some things done. But as we discovered, this was not very clever. The interest charged just grew and grew. And although we didn't have to worry about paying anything back, it would fall onto our children to sort it out.

Home 14

So, you've guessed it, we put our house on the market and sold very quickly. We then bought a three-bedroom semi-detached cottage, where we have been living, just the two us, for the last six years. Debt free—*totally*!